THE LANGUAGE OF FLOWERS

Vernon Coleman

BOOKS BY VERNON COLEMAN

The Medicine Men (1975)
Paper Doctors (1976)
Everything You Want To Know About Ageing (1976)
Stress Control (1978)
The Home Pharmacy (1980)
Aspirin or Ambulance (1980)
Face Values (1981)
Guilt (1982)
The Good Medicine Guide (1982)
Stress And Your Stomach (1983)
Bodypower (1983)
An A to Z Of Women's Problems (1984)
Bodysense (1984)
Taking Care Of Your Skin (1984)
Life Without Tranquillisers (1985)
High Blood Pressure (1985)
Diabetes (1985)
Arthritis (1985)
Eczema and Dermatitis (1985)
The Story Of Medicine (1985)
Natural Pain Control (1986)
Mindpower (1986)
Addicts and Addictions (1986)
Dr Vernon Coleman's Guide To Alternative Medicine (1988)
Stress Management Techniques (1988)
Overcoming Stress (1988)
Know Yourself (1988)
The Health Scandal (1988)
The 20 Minute Health Check (1989)
Sex For Everyone (1989)
Mind Over Body (1989)
Eat Green Lose Weight (1990)
Toxic Stress (1991)
Why Animal Experiments Must Stop (1991)
The Drugs Myth (1992)
Why Doctors Do More Harm Than Good (1993)
Stress and Relaxation (1993)
Complete Guide to Sex (1993)
How to Conquer Backache (1993)
How to Conquer Arthritis (1993)
Betrayal of Trust (1994)
Know Your Drugs (1994)
Food for Thought (1994)
The Traditional Home Doctor (1994)
I Hope Your Penis Shrivels Up (1994)
People Watching (1995)
Relief from IBS (1995)

The Parent's Handbook (1995)
Oral Sex: Bad Taste And Hard To Swallow (1995)
Why Is Pubic Hair Curly? (1995)
Power over Cancer (1996)
Men in Dresses (1996)
How to Stop Your Doctor Killing You (1996)
How to Conquer Arthritis (1996 rev)

novels
The Village Cricket Tour (1990)
The Bilbury Chronicles (1992)
Bilbury Grange (1993)
Mrs Caldicot's Cabbage War (1993)
The Man Who Inherited a Golf Course (1993)
Bilbury Revels (1994)
Deadline (1994)
Bilbury Country (1996)

short stories
Bilbury Pie (1995)

on cricket
Thomas Winsden's Cricketing Almanack (1983)
Diary Of A Cricket Lover (1984)

as Edward Vernon
Practice Makes Perfect (1977)
Practise What You Preach (1978)
Getting Into Practice (1979)
Aphrodisiacs - An Owners Manual (1983)
Aphrodisiacs - An Owners Manual (Turbo Edition) (1984)
The Complete Guide To Life (1984)

as Marc Charbonnier
Tunnel (novel 1980)

with Dr Alan C Turin
No More Headaches (1981)

with Alice
Alice's Diary (1989)
Alice's Adventures (1992)

THE LANGUAGE OF FLOWERS

Edited by

Vernon Coleman

Chilton Designs Publishers

First published 1973 by Chilton Designs Limited. This revised edition published in 1996 by Chilton Designs Publishers, Publishing House, Trinity Place, Barnstaple, North Devon, EX32 9HJ, England.

ISBN: 1-898146-25 X

A catalogue record for this book is available from the British Library.

Printed and bound by: Printers of Barnstaple.

Foreword to the 1996 edition.

It is over twenty years since I first published this edition of 'The Language of Flowers'. It was my first 'book' and I was thrilled that it gave so much pleasure to so many people. For years afterwards people wrote to me asking for copies. I'm delighted to be able to publish this edition especially for customers of Chilton Designs Publishers.

Vernon Coleman, North Devon 1996

INTRODUCTION

The red rose, we all know, is a symbol of love. But how many people know that if they give someone a garden daisy they are really saying "I share your sentiments"?

The bilberry denotes treachery, the snowdrop hope and the bluebell constancy. The ivy is the symbol of friendship, the mandrake means horror and if someone hands you a lettuce they're telling you that they think you are cold hearted!

The original version of the Language of Flowers reproduced in this small book was first published in 1852. At that time it was common for citizens to express their sentiments with the aid of flowers and a small bouquet could be used to start a spirited conversation.

In an age when people fill their homes with plastic flowers and when fields once bright with flowers are now decorated with deadly ribbons of tarmacadam and streams of pylons marching across the countryside like so many giant matchstick men it is comforting to remember something as frothy and decorative as the Language of Flowers.

It is a pleasantly useless subject with no political, social, academic or commercial raison d'être. It exists purely for fun, to enable us to pick a bunch of flowers which contains a poem. To give us a private code with great style.

Vernon Coleman, Inkpen, Berks 1973

FLOWERS
AND THEIR MEANINGS

Acacia	Chaste love
Acacia, rose	Platonic love; Friendship
Acacia, yellow	Secret love
Acacia, pink	Elegance
Agnus Castus	Indifference; Coldness
Agrimony	Thankfulness
Almond Tree	Stupidity; Indiscretion
Aloe	Grief
Amaranth	Immortality
Amaranth, Globe	Unchangeable
Amarylis	Timidity
Ambrosia	Love returned
Anemone, garden	Forsaken
Anemone, field	Sickness
Angelica	Inspiration
Apple	Temptation
Apple Blossom	Preference
Apple, thorn	Deceitful charms
Arum or Wake Robin	Ardour
Ash Tree	Grandeur
Ash, mountain	Prudence
Aspen Tree	Lamentation
Auricula	Painting
Auricula, scarlet	Avarice
Azalea	Temperance
Balm	Sympathy
Balm, gentle	Pleasantry
Balsam	Impatience; Ardent Love
Barberry	Sourness; Sharpness
Basil, sweet	Hatred
Bay Tree	Glory

Berry Wreath	Reward of Merit
Bearded Crepis	Protection
Bee Orphrys	Error
Beech Tree	Prosperity
Belladonna	Silence
Betony	Surprise
Bilberry	Treachery
Birch Tree	Meekness
Bindweed, great	Insinuation
Bindweed, small	Humility
Black Thorn	Difficulty
Bladder Nut Tree	Amusement
Blae Berry	Simplicity
Blue Bell	Constancy
Blue Bottle (Centaury)	Delicacy
Bonus Henricus	Goodness
Box	Stoicism
Borage	Bluntness
Bramble	Lowliness; Envy
Bullrush	Docility
Burdock	Touch me not
Broom	Neatness; Humility
Buttercup	Childishness; Ingratitude
Butterfly Orchis	Gaiety
Cabbage	Gain
Cactus	Horror
Calycanthus	Compassion; Benevolence
Camellia Japonica	Pity
Canary Grass	Perseverance
Canterbury Bell	Gratitude
Candytuft	Indifference

Carnation	Woman's love
Carnation, stripped	Refusal
Carnation, yellow	Disdain
Catchfly	Pretended love
Catchfly, red	Youthful love
Catchfly, white	Betrayed
Cedar Leaf	I live for thee
Cedar of Lebanon	Incorruptible
Cedar Tree	Strength; Constancy
Celandine	Joys to come
Chamomile	Energy in adversity
Cherry Tree, white	Deception
Chestnut	Luxury
Chestnut Tree	Do me justice
Chickweed	Rendezvous
Chicory	Frugality
China Aster	Variety
China Aster, single	I will think of it
Chrysanthemum, China	Cheerfulness in misfortune
Chrysanthemum, red	I love
Chrysanthemum, white	Truth
Chrysanthemum, yellow	Slighted love
Cinqurfoil	Maternal affection
Clematis	Mental beauty
Clematis, evergreen	Poverty; Artifice
Clover	Dignity
Clover, red	Industry
Coltsfoot	Justice shall be done
Columbine	Folly; Frivolity
Columbine, purple	Resolution; Desertion
Columbine, red	Anxious

Convolvulus	Uncertainty
Convolvulus, major	Extinguished hope
Convolvulus, minor	Night
Coriander	Concealed merit
Coreopsis	Always cheerful
Coreopsis, arkansa	Love at first sight
Corn	Riches
Corn-bottle	Delicacy
Cowslip	Pensiveness; Winning Grace
Cowslip, American	You are my divinity
Cranberry	Cure for heartache
Crane's Bill	Envy
Cresses	Stability
Crocus	Abuse not
Crocus, Spring	Youthful gladness
Cudweed (Everlasting)	Never-ceasing Remembrance
Cucumber	Criticism
Currants	You please all
Cypress	Death; Mourning
Cypress and Marigold	Despair; Melancholy
Daffodil	Chivalry
Daffodil, great yellow	Regard
Dahlia	Elegance and dignity
Daisy	Cheerfulness
Daisy, double	Participation
Daisy, Ox-Eye	A token
Daisy, red	Unconscious
Daisy, white	Innocence
Daisy, garden	I share your sentiments
Daisy, wild	I will think of it
Dandelion	Love's oracle
Darnel	Wickedness

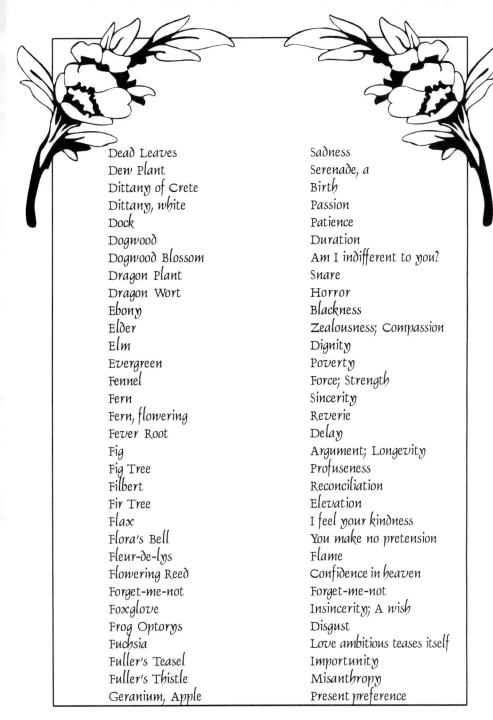

Dead Leaves	Sadness
Dew Plant	Serenade, a
Dittany of Crete	Birth
Dittany, white	Passion
Dock	Patience
Dogwood	Duration
Dogwood Blossom	Am I indifferent to you?
Dragon Plant	Snare
Dragon Wort	Horror
Ebony	Blackness
Elder	Zealousness; Compassion
Elm	Dignity
Evergreen	Poverty
Fennel	Force; Strength
Fern	Sincerity
Fern, flowering	Reverie
Fever Root	Delay
Fig	Argument; Longevity
Fig Tree	Profuseness
Filbert	Reconciliation
Fir Tree	Elevation
Flax	I feel your kindness
Flora's Bell	You make no pretension
Fleur-de-lys	Flame
Flowering Reed	Confidence in heaven
Forget-me-not	Forget-me-not
Foxglove	Insincerity; A wish
Frog Optorys	Disgust
Fuchsia	Love ambitious teases itself
Fuller's Teasel	Importunity
Fuller's Thistle	Misanthropy
Geranium, Apple	Present preference

Geranium	Gentility
Geranium, Crane's Bill	Envy
Geranium, Nutmeg	An expected meeting
Geranium, rose or pink	Preference
Geranium, scarlet	Comforting; Stupidity
Geranium, silver-leaved	Recall
Geranium, pencil-leaved	Ingenuity
Geranium, wild	Steadfast piety
Gilly Flower	Unfading beauty
Goat's Rue	Reason
Golden Rod	Precaution; Encouragement
Gooseberry	Anticipation
Gorse	Enduring affection
Grass	Submission; Desolation
Harebell	Grief
Hawkweed	Quick-sightedness
Hawthorn	Hope
Hazel	Reconciliation
Heath	Solitude
Helenium	Tears
Heliotrope	Devotion; Faithfulness
Hellebore	Scandal
Hemlock	You will be my death
Hemp	Fate
Hanbane	Defect
Hepatica (Linwort)	Confidence
Hibiscus	Delicate beauty
Holly	Am I forgotten?
Holly Herb	Enchantment
Hollyhock, white	Female ambition
Hollyhock	Fertility

Honesty (Lunaria)	Fascination
Honey Flower	Love sweet and secret
Honeysuckle, French	Rustic beauty
Honeysuckle, coral	The colour of my fate
Honeysuckle, monthly	Bond of love
Honeysuckle, wild	Inconstancy of love
Hop	Injustice
Horehound	Fire
Hortensia	You are cold
Houseleek	Vivacity
Houstonia	Content
Hyacinth	Jealousy
Hyacinth, blue	Constancy
Hyacinth, purple	Sorrow
Hydrangea	A boaster; Heartlessness
Hyssop	Cleanliness
Iceland Moss	Health
Imperial Montague	Power
Iris	My compliments
Iris, yellow	Flame; Passion
Ivy	Friendship; Matrimony
Ivy, sprig with tendrils	Assiduous to please
Jasmine, Cape	Transport of joy
Jasmine, Indian	I attach myself to you
Jasmine, Spanish	Sensuality
Jasmine, white	Amiability
Jasmine, Virginian	Separation
Jasmine, yellow	Grace and elegance
Jonquil	I desire a return of affection
Judas Tree	Betrayal; Unbelief
Juniper	Succour; Protection

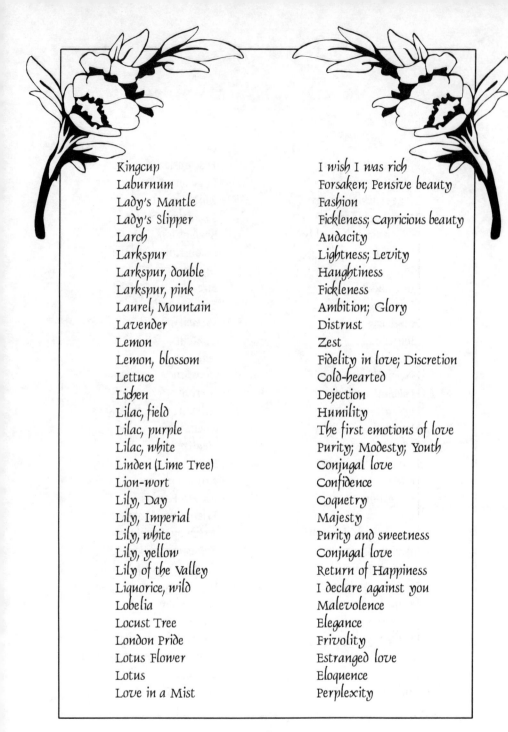

Kingcup	I wish I was rich
Laburnum	Forsaken; Pensive beauty
Lady's Mantle	Fashion
Lady's Slipper	Fickleness; Capricious beauty
Larch	Audacity
Larkspur	Lightness; Levity
Larkspur, double	Haughtiness
Larkspur, pink	Fickleness
Laurel, Mountain	Ambition; Glory
Lavender	Distrust
Lemon	Zest
Lemon, blossom	Fidelity in love; Discretion
Lettuce	Cold-hearted
Lichen	Dejection
Lilac, field	Humility
Lilac, purple	The first emotions of love
Lilac, white	Purity; Modesty; Youth
Linden (Lime Tree)	Conjugal love
Lion-wort	Confidence
Lily, Day	Coquetry
Lily, Imperial	Majesty
Lily, white	Purity and sweetness
Lily, yellow	Conjugal love
Lily of the Valley	Return of Happiness
Liquorice, wild	I declare against you
Lobelia	Malevolence
Locust Tree	Elegance
London Pride	Frivolity
Lotus Flower	Estranged love
Lotus	Eloquence
Love in a Mist	Perplexity

Love in a Puzzle	Embarrassment
Love-lies-bleeding	Hopeless not heartless
Lozenge-leaved Boubon	Concealment
Lythrum	Pretension
Lucern	Life
Lupine	Voraciousness; Imagination
Madder	Calumny
Madwort	Tranquillity
Magnolia	Love of nature
Magnolia, Swamp	Perseverance
Maiden Hair	Discretion; Secrecy
Maize	Plenty
Mallow, Marsh	Mild disposition; Beneficence
Mallow, Syrian	Consumed by love
Mallow, Venetian	Delicate beauty
Manchineel	Hypocrisy
Mandrake	Horror
Maple	Reserve
Majoram	Blushes
Marvel of Peru	Timidity
Marigold	Chagrin; Pain; Cruelty
Marigold, African	Vulgar minded
Marigold, Fig	Idleness
Marigold, French	Jealousy
Marigold, Garden	Uneasiness; Grief
Meadow, Lychnis	Wit
Meadow Saffron	My best days are past
Meadow Sweet	Uselessness
Mesembryanthemum	Laziness
Mezerion	I desire to please
Milkvetch	Your presence revives me

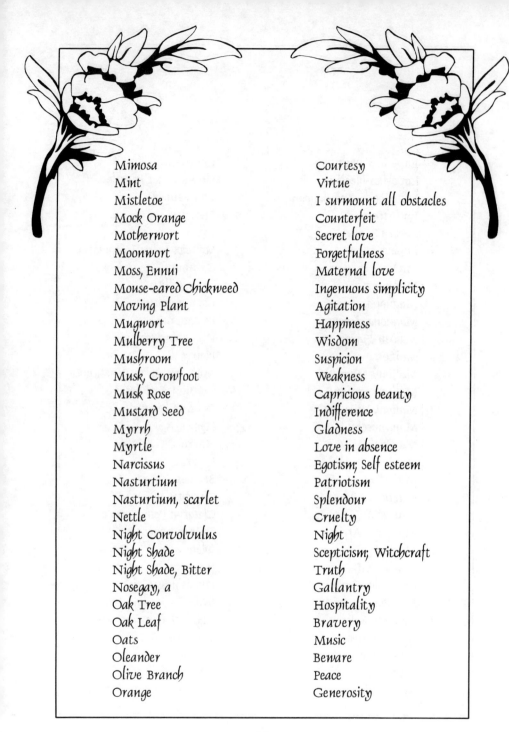

Mimosa	Courtesy
Mint	Virtue
Mistletoe	I surmount all obstacles
Mock Orange	Counterfeit
Motherwort	Secret love
Moonwort	Forgetfulness
Moss, Ennui	Maternal love
Mouse-eared Chickweed	Ingenuous simplicity
Moving Plant	Agitation
Mugwort	Happiness
Mulberry Tree	Wisdom
Mushroom	Suspicion
Musk, Crowfoot	Weakness
Musk Rose	Capricious beauty
Mustard Seed	Indifference
Myrrh	Gladness
Myrtle	Love in absence
Narcissus	Egotism; Self esteem
Nasturtium	Patriotism
Nasturtium, scarlet	Splendour
Nettle	Cruelty
Night Convolvulus	Night
Night Shade	Scepticism; Witchcraft
Night Shade, Bitter	Truth
Nosegay, a	Gallantry
Oak Tree	Hospitality
Oak Leaf	Bravery
Oats	Music
Oleander	Beware
Olive Branch	Peace
Orange	Generosity

Orchis	A beauty
Osier	Frankness
Osmunda	Dreams
Ox-Eye	Penitence
Palm	Victory
Pansy (Heartsease)	You occupy my thoughts
Passion Flower	Belief; Susceptibility
Pea, Sweet	Departure
Peach Blossom	I am your captive
Pear Tree	Affection
Penny Royal	Flee away
Peony	Anger; A frown
Peppermint	Warmth; Cordiality
Periwinkle, white	Pleasant recollections
Periwinkle, blue	Pleasures of memory
Periwinkle, red	Early friendship
Pine Apple	Perfection
Pine, black	Pity
Pine, Spruce	Farewell; Hope in adversity
Pink	Boldness
Pink, Carnation	Woman's love
Pink, Indian double	Always lovely
Pink, Indian single	Aversion
Pink, Mountain	You are aspiring
Pink, red double	Pure, ardent love
Pink, variegated	Refusal
Pink, white	You are fair and fascinating
Pink, yellow	Disdain
Pimpernel	Change
Plane Tree	Genius
Plum Tree, wild	Independence

Polyanthus	Pride of riches
Polyanthus, crimson	The heart's mystery
Polyanthus, lilac	Confidence
Pomegranate	Foolishness
Pompon Rose	Gentility; Prettiness
Poplar	Courage
Poppy	Fleeting pleasure
Poppy, red	Consolation
Poppy, scarlet	Fantastic
Potato	Beneficence
Prickly Pear	Satire
Pride of China	Dissension
Primrose, early	Youth
Primrose, evening	Inconstancy
Privet	Defence; Mildness
Pyramidal Bell Flower	Gratitude
Quaking Grass	Agitation
Quamoclit	Busybody
Quince	Temptation
Ragged Robin	Wit
Ranunculus	I am dazzled by your charms
Ranunculus, garden	You are rich in attraction
Ranunculus, wild	Ingratitude
Raspberry	Remorse
Redbay	Love; Memory
Red Catchfly	Youthful love
Reeds	Music
Reeds, split	Indication
Rhododendron	Danger
Rhubarb	Advice
Rocket	Rivalry

24

Rosebay	Beware
Rose, Austrian	Thou art all that is lovely
Rose, bridal	Happy love
Rose, burgundy	Unconscious
Rose, cabbage	Ambassador
Rose, Carolina	Love is dangerous
Rose, China	Grace
Rose, Christmas	Tranquillize my anxiety
Rose, Damask	Freshness
Rose, deep red	Bashful shame
Rose, dog	Pleasure and pain
Rose, hundred-leaved	Pride
Rose, Japan	Pity
Rose, Lancaster	Union
Rose, May	Precocity
Rose, moss, bud	Confession of love
Rose, moss, full	Superior merit
Rose, Mundi	You are merry
Rose, musk	Capricious beauty
Rose, musk, cluster	Charming
Rose, red, bud	You are young and beautiful
Rose, red-leaved	Beauty and prosperity
Rose, red, full	Beauty
Rose, unique	Call me not beautiful
Rose, white, bud	A heart ignorant of love
Rose, white, full	I am worthy of your love
Rose, yellow	Decrease of love
Rose, York	War
Rose, white and red together	Unity
Roses, crown made of	Reward of virtue
Rosemary	Remembrance

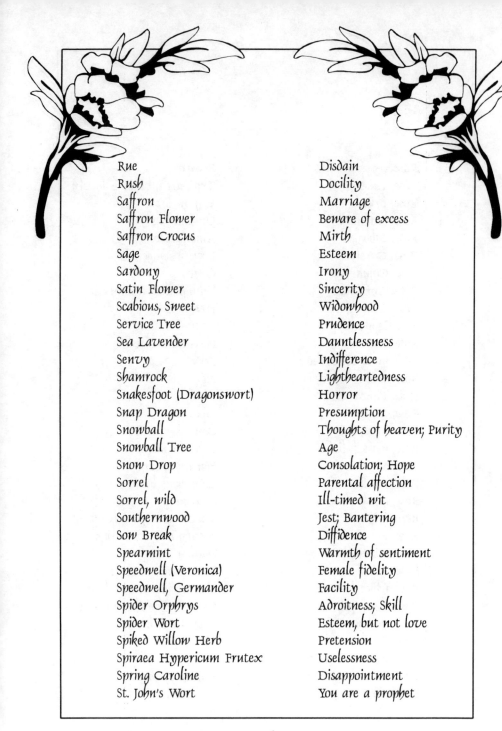

Rue	Disdain
Rush	Docility
Saffron	Marriage
Saffron Flower	Beware of excess
Saffron Crocus	Mirth
Sage	Esteem
Sardony	Irony
Satin Flower	Sincerity
Scabious, Sweet	Widowhood
Service Tree	Prudence
Sea Lavender	Dauntlessness
Senvy	Indifference
Shamrock	Lightheartedness
Snakesfoot (Dragonswort)	Horror
Snap Dragon	Presumption
Snowball	Thoughts of heaven; Purity
Snowball Tree	Age
Snow Drop	Consolation; Hope
Sorrel	Parental affection
Sorrel, wild	Ill-timed wit
Southernwood	Jest; Bantering
Sow Break	Diffidence
Spearmint	Warmth of sentiment
Speedwell (Veronica)	Female fidelity
Speedwell, Germander	Facility
Spider Orphrys	Adroitness; Skill
Spider Wort	Esteem, but not love
Spiked Willow Herb	Pretension
Spiraea Hypericum Frutex	Uselessness
Spring Caroline	Disappointment
St. John's Wort	You are a prophet

Stock, ten week	Promptitude
Stonecrop	Tranquillity
Straw, broken	Rupture
Strawberry	Perfect excellence
Strawberry Tree	Esteem and love
Sunflower, dwarf	Adoration
Sunflower, tall	Haughtiness
Swalloa Wort	Cure for heartache
Sweet Briar	Simplicity
Sweet Briar, yellow	Decrease of love
Sweet Flag	Fitness
Sweet Pea	Departure
Sweet Sultan Flower	Widowhood
Sweet William	Gallantry; Finess; A smile
Sycamore	Curiosity
Syringa	Memory
Syringa Carolina	Disappointment
Tamarisk	Crime
Tansey	I declare against you
Tiger Flower	May pride befriend me
Thistle, common	Austerity
Thistle, Scotch	Retaliation
Thorns, bunch of	Severity
Thrift	Sympathy
Throutwort	Neglected beauty
Thyme	Thriftiness
Touch-me-not	Impatient resolves
Traveller's Joy	Safety
Tremella Nestoc	Resistance
Trefoil	Revenge
Truffle	Surprise

Tuber-Rose	Dangerous pleasures
Tulip	Fame
Tulip, red	Declaration of love
Tulip, variegated	Beautiful eyes
Tulip, yellow	Hopeless love
Turnip	Charity
Valerian	Accommodating disposition
Venus's looking-glass	Flattery
Veronica	Fidelity in friendship
Vervain	Enchantment
Vetch	Shyness
Violet, blue	Faithfulness; Love
Violet, purple	You occupy my thoughts
Violet, white	Innocence; Modesty
Violet, wild	Love in idleness
Vine	Drunkenness
Wallflower	Fidelity in misfortune
Wheat	Prosperity
Whin	Anger
White Bell Flower	Gratitude
Willow, water	Freedom
Willow Herb	Pretension
Willow, Weeping	Melancholy
Wood Sorrel	Joy
Wormwood	Absence
Yew	Sadness
Zephyr Flower	Expectation

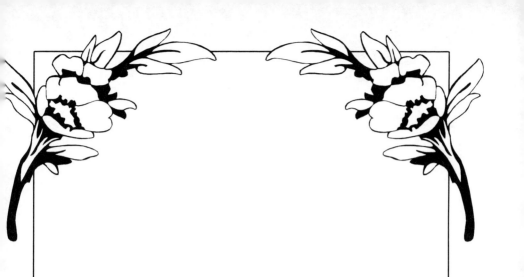

FLOWERS
BY DEFINITION

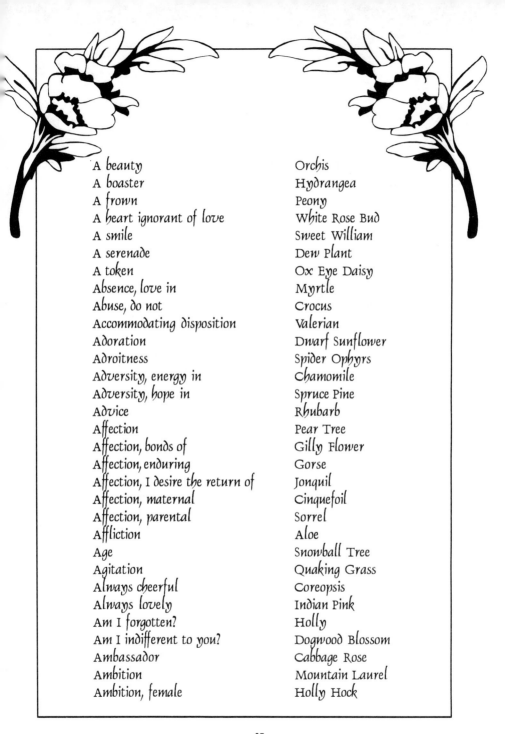

A beauty	Orchis
A boaster	Hydrangea
A frown	Peony
A heart ignorant of love	White Rose Bud
A smile	Sweet William
A serenade	Dew Plant
A token	Ox Eye Daisy
Absence, love in	Myrtle
Abuse, do not	Crocus
Accommodating disposition	Valerian
Adoration	Dwarf Sunflower
Adroitness	Spider Ophyrs
Adversity, energy in	Chamomile
Adversity, hope in	Spruce Pine
Advice	Rhubarb
Affection	Pear Tree
Affection, bonds of	Gilly Flower
Affection, enduring	Gorse
Affection, I desire the return of	Jonquil
Affection, maternal	Cinquefoil
Affection, parental	Sorrel
Affliction	Aloe
Age	Snowball Tree
Agitation	Quaking Grass
Always cheerful	Coreopsis
Always lovely	Indian Pink
Am I forgotten?	Holly
Am I indifferent to you?	Dogwood Blossom
Ambassador	Cabbage Rose
Ambition	Mountain Laurel
Ambition, female	Holly Hock

Ambitious love teases itself	Fuchsia
Amiability	White Jasmine
Amusement	Bladder Nut Tree
An expected meeting	Nutmeg Geranium
Anger	Peony
Anticipation	Gooseberry
Anxiety, tranquillize my	Christmas Rose
Anxious and trembling	Red Columbine
Ardent love	Balsam
Ardour	Arum
Argument	Fig
Artifice	Evergreen Clematis
Aspiring, you are	Mountain Pink
Assiduous to please	Ivy Sprig
Attractions, you are rich in	Garden Ranunculas
Audacity	Larch
Austerity	Common Thistle
Avarice	Scarlet Auricula
Aversion	Indian Pink
Bantering	Southernwood
Bashful shame	Deep Red Rose
Beautiful, call me not	Unique Rose
Beautiful eyes	Variegated Tulip
Beautiful, you are young and	Red Rose Bud
Beauty, a	Orchis
Beauty and prosperity	Red-leaved Rose
Beauty, capricious	Lady's Slipper; Musk Rose
Beauty, delicate	Hibiscus
Beauty, mental	Clematis
Beauty, neglected	Throutwort
Beauty, pensive	Laburnum

Beauty, rustic	French Honeysuckle
Beauty, unfading	Gilly Flower
Belief	Passion Flower
Belle, a	Orchis
Benevolence	Calycanthus
Betrayal	Judas Tree
Betrayed	White Catchfly
Beware of excess	Saffron Flower
Beware	Oleander; Rosebay
Birth	Dittany of Crete
Blackness	Ebony
Bluntness	Borage
Boaster, a	Hydrangea
Boldness	Pink
Bond of affection	Gilly Flower
Bond of love	Honeysuckle
Bravery and humanity	Oak Leaf
Busybody	Quamoclit
Call me not beautiful	Unique Rose
Capricious beauty	Musk Rose; Lady's Slipper
Captive, I am your	Peach Blossom
Charming	Cluster of Musk Rose
Charms, deceitful	Apple Thorn
Charms, I am dazzled by your	Ranunculus
Charity	Turnip
Chaste love	Acacia
Chastity	Orange Blossom
Cheerful always	Coreopsis
Cheerfulness	Daisy
Cheerfulness under misfortune	Chrysanthemum
Childishness	Buttercup

Chivalry	Daffodil
Cleanliness	Hyssop
Cold, you are	Hortensia
Cold-hearted	Lettuce
Coldness	Agnus Castus
Concealed merit	Coriander
Confession of love	Moss Rose-bud
Confidence	Hepatica; Lilac Polyanthus
Confidence in heaven	Flowering Reed
Conjugal love	Linden
Consolation	Snowdrop; Poppy
Constancy	Cedar Tree; Blue Hyacinth
Consumed by love	Althea Frutex
Content	Houstonia
Comforting	Scarlet Geranium
Compassion	Calycanthus; Elder
Compliments, my	Iris
Cordiality	Peppermint
Coquetry	Day Lily
Counterfeit	Mock Orange
Courage	Poplar
Criticism	Cucumber
Cruelty	Nettle; Marigold
Curiosity	Sycamore
Danger	Rhododendron
Dangerous, love is	Carolina Rose
Dark thoughts	Night Shade
Dauntlessness	Sea Lavender
Death	Cypress
Death, I change but in	Bay Leaf
Death, you will be my	Hemlock
Deceit	Dogvane

Deceitful charms	Apple Thorn
Deception	White Cherry Tree
Declaration of love	Tulip
Decrease of love	Yellow Rose
Defect	Henbane
Defence	Privet
Dejection	Lichen
Delicacy	Cornbottle; Blue Bottle
Delicate beauty	Flower-of-an-hour
Departure	Sweet Pea
Desertion	Purple Columbine
Desolation	Grass
Despair	Cypress and Marigold
Devotion	Heliotrope
Difficulty	Black Thorn
Diffidence	Sowbread
Dignity	Clover; Elm
Dignity, elegance and	Dahlia
Disappointed expectation	Fish Geranium
Disappointment	Spring Caroline
Discretion	Lemon Blossom
Disdain	Yellow Pink; Rue
Disgust	Frog Optorys
Disposition, accommodating	Valerian
Dissension	Pride of China
Distrust	Lavender
Divinity, you are my	American Cowslip
Do me justice	Chestnut Tree
Do not abuse	Saffron Flower
Docility	Bullrush
Domestic Happiness	Honeysuckle
Dreams	Osmunda

Drunkenness	Vine
Durability	Cherry Tree
Duration	Dogwood
Early Friendship	Red Periwinkle
Egotism	Narcissus
Elegance	Pink Acacia
Elegance and dignity	Dahlia
Elegance, grace and	Yellow Jasmine
Enchantment	Vervain; Holly
Encouragement	Golden Rod
Enduring affection	Gorse
Energy in adversity	Chamomile
Ennui	Moss
Envy	Crane's Bill; Bramble
Error	Bee Orphrys
Esteem	Sage
Esteem and love	Strawberry Tree
Esteem, but not love	Spiderwort
Estranged love	Lotus Flower
Evanescent pleasure	Poppy
Excellence, perfect	Strawberry
Excess, beware of	Saffron Flower
Expectation	Zephyr Flower
Extinguished hope	Convolvulus
Eyes, beautiful	Variegated Tulip
Facility	Germander Speedwell
Faithfulness	Heliotrope
Falsehood	Yellow Lily
Fame	Tulip
Fantastic	Scarlet Poppy
Farewell	Spruce Pine

Fascinating, you are fair and	White Pink
Fascination	Honesty
Fashion	Lady's Mantle
Fashionable	Queen's Rocket
Fate	Hemp
Fertility	Hollyhock
Female ambition	White Hollyhock
Female fidelity	Speedwell
Fickleness	Abatina; Lady's Slipper
Fidelity	Ivy
Fidelity, female	Speedwell
Fidelity in friendship	Veronica
Fidelity in love	Lemon Blossom
Fidelity in misfortune	Wallflower
Filial love	Virgin's Bower
Finesse	Sweet William
Fire	Horehound
First sight, love at	Arkansa Coreopsis
Flame	Yellow Iris; Fleur de lys
Flattery	Venus's Looking-glass
Fleeting Pleasure	Poppy
Flee away	Penny Royal
Folly	Columbine
Foolishness	Pomegranate
For once may pride befriend me	Tiger Flower
Force	Fennel
Foresight	Holly
Forgetfulness	Moonwort
Forget-me-not	Forget-me-not
Forsaken	Garden Anemone
Frankness	Osier

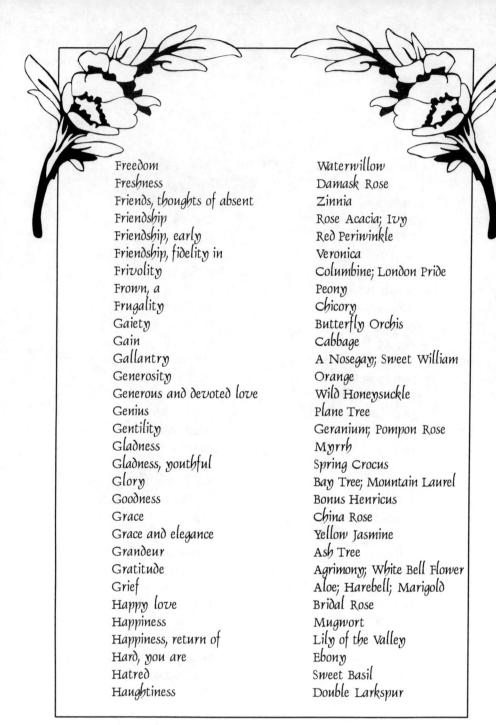

Freedom	Waterwillow
Freshness	Damask Rose
Friends, thoughts of absent	Zinnia
Friendship	Rose Acacia; Ivy
Friendship, early	Red Periwinkle
Friendship, fidelity in	Veronica
Frivolity	Columbine; London Pride
Frown, a	Peony
Frugality	Chicory
Gaiety	Butterfly Orchis
Gain	Cabbage
Gallantry	A Nosegay; Sweet William
Generosity	Orange
Generous and devoted love	Wild Honeysuckle
Genius	Plane Tree
Gentility	Geranium; Pompon Rose
Gladness	Myrrh
Gladness, youthful	Spring Crocus
Glory	Bay Tree; Mountain Laurel
Goodness	Bonus Henricus
Grace	China Rose
Grace and elegance	Yellow Jasmine
Grandeur	Ash Tree
Gratitude	Agrimony; White Bell Flower
Grief	Aloe; Harebell; Marigold
Happy love	Bridal Rose
Happiness	Mugwort
Happiness, return of	Lily of the Valley
Hard, you are	Ebony
Hatred	Sweet Basil
Haughtiness	Double Larkspur

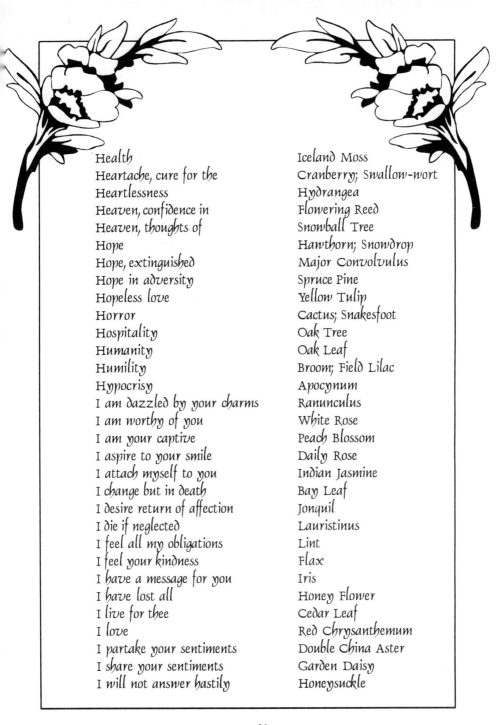

Health	Iceland Moss
Heartache, cure for the	Cranberry; Swallow-wort
Heartlessness	Hydrangea
Heaven, confidence in	Flowering Reed
Heaven, thoughts of	Snowball Tree
Hope	Hawthorn; Snowdrop
Hope, extinguished	Major Convolvulus
Hope in adversity	Spruce Pine
Hopeless love	Yellow Tulip
Horror	Cactus; Snakesfoot
Hospitality	Oak Tree
Humanity	Oak Leaf
Humility	Broom; Field Lilac
Hypocrisy	Apocynum
I am dazzled by your charms	Ranunculus
I am worthy of you	White Rose
I am your captive	Peach Blossom
I aspire to your smile	Daily Rose
I attach myself to you	Indian Jasmine
I change but in death	Bay Leaf
I desire return of affection	Jonquil
I die if neglected	Lauristinus
I feel all my obligations	Lint
I feel your kindness	Flax
I have a message for you	Iris
I have lost all	Honey Flower
I live for thee	Cedar Leaf
I love	Red Chrysanthemum
I partake your sentiments	Double China Aster
I share your sentiments	Garden Daisy
I will not answer hastily	Honeysuckle

I will think of it	China Aster
I wish I was rich	Kingcup
Idleness, love in	Wild Violet
Ill-temper	Barberry
Ill-timed wit	Wild Sorrel
Immortality	Amaranth
Impatience	Balsam
Impatient resolves	Touch-me-not
Inconstancy	Evening Primrose
Inconstancy in love	Wild Honeysuckle
Incorruptible	Cedar of Lebanon
Independence	Wild Plum Tree
Indication	Split Reeds
Indifference	Candytuft
Indiscretion	Almond Tree
Industry	Red Clover
Ingenuity	Pencil-leafed Geranium
Ingenuous simplicity	Mouse-eared Chickweed
Ingratitude	Buttercup
Injustice	Hop
Innocence	White Daisy; White Violet
Insincerity	Foxglove
Insinuation	Great Bindweed
Inspiration	Angelica
Irony	Sardony
Jealousy	Hyacinth; Marigold
Jest	Southernwood
Joy	Wood Sorrel
Joys to come	Celandine
Justice, do me	Chestnut Tree
Justice shall be done	Coltsfoot

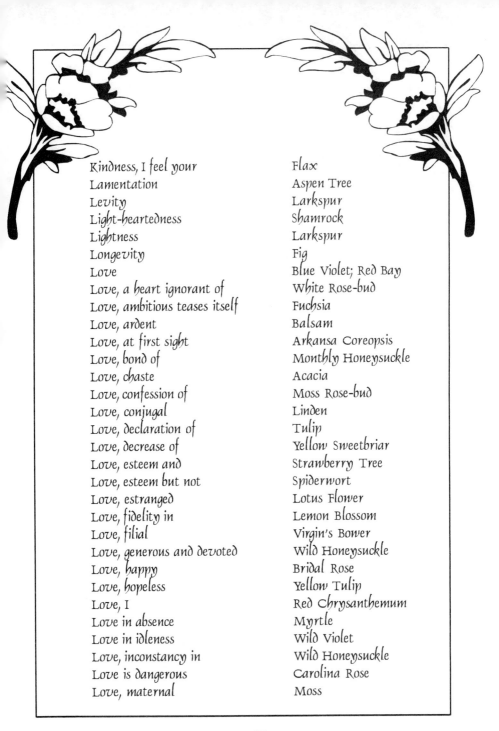

Kindness, I feel your	Flax
Lamentation	Aspen Tree
Levity	Larkspur
Light-heartedness	Shamrock
Lightness	Larkspur
Longevity	Fig
Love	Blue Violet; Red Bay
Love, a heart ignorant of	White Rose-bud
Love, ambitious teases itself	Fuchsia
Love, ardent	Balsam
Love, at first sight	Arkansa Coreopsis
Love, bond of	Monthly Honeysuckle
Love, chaste	Acacia
Love, confession of	Moss Rose-bud
Love, conjugal	Linden
Love, declaration of	Tulip
Love, decrease of	Yellow Sweetbriar
Love, esteem and	Strawberry Tree
Love, esteem but not	Spiderwort
Love, estranged	Lotus Flower
Love, fidelity in	Lemon Blossom
Love, filial	Virgin's Bower
Love, generous and devoted	Wild Honeysuckle
Love, happy	Bridal Rose
Love, hopeless	Yellow Tulip
Love, I	Red Chrysanthemum
Love in absence	Myrtle
Love in idleness	Wild Violet
Love, inconstancy in	Wild Honeysuckle
Love is dangerous	Carolina Rose
Love, maternal	Moss

Love, only deserve my	Campion Rose
Love, platonic	Rose Acacia
Love, pretended	Catchfly
Love, pure and ardent	Red Pink
Love, returned	Ambrosia
Love, secret	Acacia
Love, slighted	Yellow Chrysanthemum
Love, sweet and secret	Honey Flower
Love, the first emotions	Purple Lilac
Love, transient	Spiderwort
Love, woman's	Carnation
Love, youthful	Red Catchfly
Lovely, always	Indian Pink
Lovely, thou art all that is	Austrian Rose
Love's oracle	Dandelion
Lowliness	Bramble
Lustre	Ranunculus
Luxury	Chestnut
Malevolence	Lobelia
Marriage	Saffron
Maternal affection	Cinquefoil
Maternal love	Moss
Matrimony	Ivy
Meekness	Birch Tree
Meeting, an appointed	Everlasting Pea
Meeting, an expected	Nutmeg Geranium
Melancholy	Cypress; Weeping Willow
Melancholy mind	Sorrowful Geranium
Memory	Red bay; Syringa
Memory, pleasures of	Blue Periwinkle
Mental beauty	Clematis; Kennedia

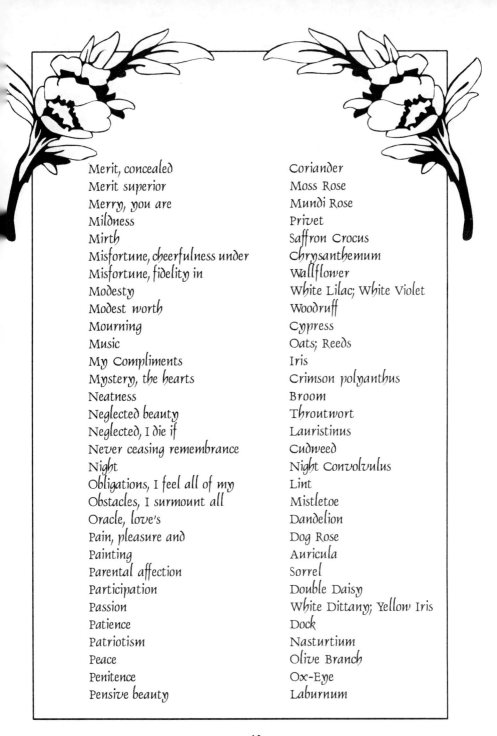

Merit, concealed	Coriander
Merit superior	Moss Rose
Merry, you are	Mundi Rose
Mildness	Privet
Mirth	Saffron Crocus
Misfortune, cheerfulness under	Chrysanthemum
Misfortune, fidelity in	Wallflower
Modesty	White Lilac; White Violet
Modest worth	Woodruff
Mourning	Cypress
Music	Oats; Reeds
My Compliments	Iris
Mystery, the hearts	Crimson polyanthus
Neatness	Broom
Neglected beauty	Throutwort
Neglected, I die if	Lauristinus
Never ceasing remembrance	Cudweed
Night	Night Convolvulus
Obligations, I feel all of my	Lint
Obstacles, I surmount all	Mistletoe
Oracle, love's	Dandelion
Pain, pleasure and	Dog Rose
Painting	Auricula
Parental affection	Sorrel
Participation	Double Daisy
Passion	White Dittany; Yellow Iris
Patience	Dock
Patriotism	Nasturtium
Peace	Olive Branch
Penitence	Ox-Eye
Pensive beauty	Laburnum

Pensiveness	Cowslip
Perfect Excellence	Strawberry
Perfection	Pine Apple
Pity	Black Pine; Japan Rose
Piety, steadfast	Wild Geranium
Platonic love	Rose Acacia
Pleasant recollections	White Periwinkle
Pleasantry	Gentle Balm
Please, assiduous to	Ivy Sprig
Pleasure and pain	Dog Rose
Pleasures, dangerous	Tuber Rose
Pleasure, fleeting	Poppy
Pleasures of memory	Blue Periwinkle
Poetry	Eglantine
Poverty	Evergreen Clematis
Power	Crown Imperial
Precaution	Golden Rod
Precocity	May Rose
Preference	Apple Blossom
Present preference	Apple Geranium
Perseverance	Canary Grass
Presumption	Snap Dragon
Pretended love	Catchfly
Pretension	Spiked Willow Herb
Pretension, you make no	Flora's Bell
Prettiness	Pompon Rose
Pride	Hundred Leaved Rose
Pride of riches	Polyanthus
Profuseness	Fig Tree
Promise, perform your	Plum Tree
Promptitude	Ten Week Stock

Prophet, you are a	St. John's Wort
Prosperity	Beech Tree; Wheat
Protection	Juniper
Prudence	Mountain Ash; Service Tree
Pure and ardent love	Red Pink
Purity	White Lilac; Snowball
Purity and sweetness	White Lily
Quick-sightedness	Hawkweed
Reason	Goat's Rue
Recall	Silver-leaved Geranium
Recluse	Moss
Recollections, pleasant	White Periwinkle
Reconciliation	Hazel; Star of Bethlehem
Refusal	Striped Carnation
Regard	Great Yellow Daffodil
Remembrance	Rosemary
Remembrance, never-ceasing	Cudweed
Remembrances, sorrowful	Adonis
Remorse	Raspberry
Rendezvous	Chickweed
Repose	Buckbean
Resemblance	Spiked Speedwell
Resistance	Tremella Nestoc
Resolution	Purple Columbine
Resolves, impatient	Touch-me-not
Retaliation	Scotch Thistle
Return of happiness	Lily of the Valley
Revenge	Trefoil
Reverie	Flowering Fern
Reward of virtue	Crown made of Roses
Rich, I wish I was	Kingcup

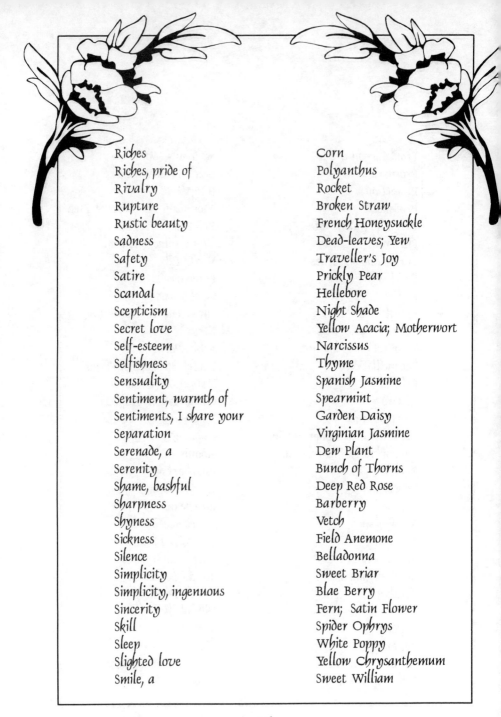

Riches	Corn
Riches, pride of	Polyanthus
Rivalry	Rocket
Rupture	Broken Straw
Rustic beauty	French Honeysuckle
Sadness	Dead-leaves; Yew
Safety	Traveller's Joy
Satire	Prickly Pear
Scandal	Hellebore
Scepticism	Night Shade
Secret love	Yellow Acacia; Motherwort
Self-esteem	Narcissus
Selfishness	Thyme
Sensuality	Spanish Jasmine
Sentiment, warmth of	Spearmint
Sentiments, I share your	Garden Daisy
Separation	Virginian Jasmine
Serenade, a	Dew Plant
Serenity	Bunch of Thorns
Shame, bashful	Deep Red Rose
Sharpness	Barberry
Shyness	Vetch
Sickness	Field Anemone
Silence	Belladonna
Simplicity	Sweet Briar
Simplicity, ingenuous	Blae Berry
Sincerity	Fern; Satin Flower
Skill	Spider Ophrys
Sleep	White Poppy
Slighted love	Yellow Chrysanthemum
Smile, a	Sweet William

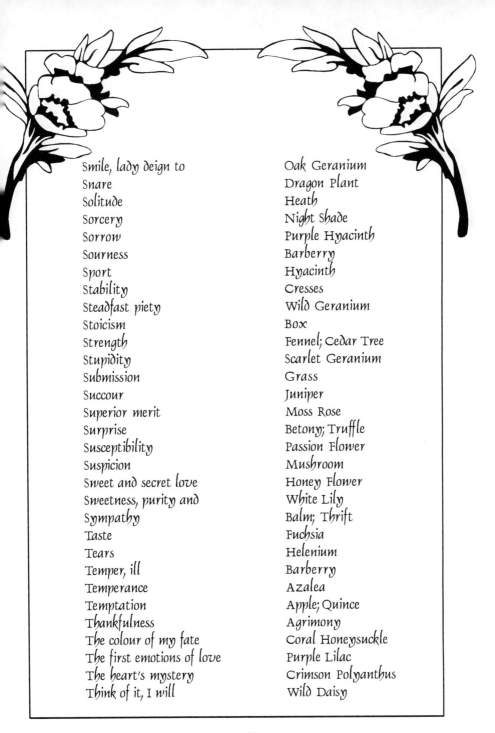

Smile, lady deign to	Oak Geranium
Snare	Dragon Plant
Solitude	Heath
Sorcery	Night Shade
Sorrow	Purple Hyacinth
Sourness	Barberry
Sport	Hyacinth
Stability	Cresses
Steadfast piety	Wild Geranium
Stoicism	Box
Strength	Fennel; Cedar Tree
Stupidity	Scarlet Geranium
Submission	Grass
Succour	Juniper
Superior merit	Moss Rose
Surprise	Betony; Truffle
Susceptibility	Passion Flower
Suspicion	Mushroom
Sweet and secret love	Honey Flower
Sweetness, purity and	White Lily
Sympathy	Balm; Thrift
Taste	Fuchsia
Tears	Helenium
Temper, ill	Barberry
Temperance	Azalea
Temptation	Apple; Quince
Thankfulness	Agrimony
The colour of my fate	Coral Honeysuckle
The first emotions of love	Purple Lilac
The heart's mystery	Crimson Polyanthus
Think of it, I will	Wild Daisy

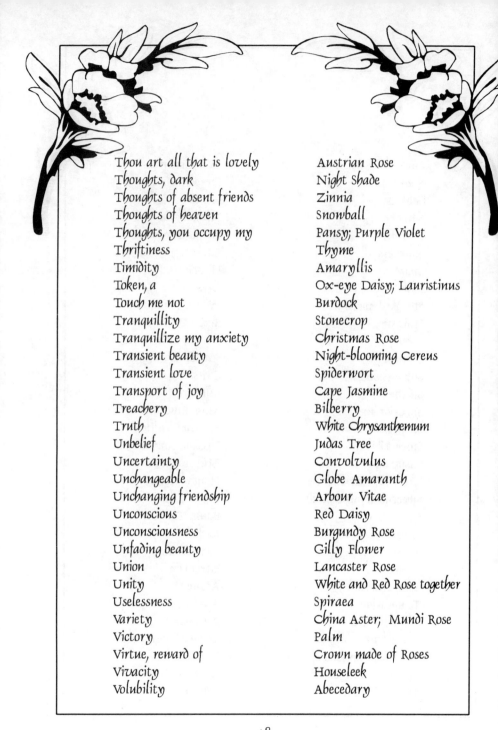

Thou art all that is lovely	Austrian Rose
Thoughts, dark	Night Shade
Thoughts of absent friends	Zinnia
Thoughts of heaven	Snowball
Thoughts, you occupy my	Pansy; Purple Violet
Thriftiness	Thyme
Timidity	Amaryllis
Token, a	Ox-eye Daisy; Lauristinus
Touch me not	Burdock
Tranquillity	Stonecrop
Tranquillize my anxiety	Christmas Rose
Transient beauty	Night-blooming Cereus
Transient love	Spiderwort
Transport of joy	Cape Jasmine
Treachery	Bilberry
Truth	White Chrysanthemum
Unbelief	Judas Tree
Uncertainty	Convolvulus
Unchangeable	Globe Amaranth
Unchanging friendship	Arbour Vitae
Unconscious	Red Daisy
Unconsciousness	Burgundy Rose
Unfading beauty	Gilly Flower
Union	Lancaster Rose
Unity	White and Red Rose together
Uselessness	Spiraea
Variety	China Aster; Mundi Rose
Victory	Palm
Virtue, reward of	Crown made of Roses
Vivacity	Houseleek
Volubility	Abecedary

War	York Rose
Warmth	Peppermint
Warmth of sentiment	Spearmint
Wickedness	Darnel
Widowhood	Sweet Sultan Flower
Wilt thou go with me?	Everlasting Pea
Winning grace	Cowslip
Wish, a	Foxglove
Wisdom	Mulberry Tree
Wit	Ragged Robin
Wit, ill-timed	Wild Sorrel
Witchcraft	Night Shade
Woman's love	Carnation
Worthy of you, I am	White Rose
You are a prophet	St. John's Wort
You are aspiring	Mountain Pink
You are cold	Hortensia
You are fair and fascinating	White Pink
You are hard	Ebony
You are merry	Mundi Rose
You are my divinity	American Cowslip
You are rich in attraction	Garden Ranunculus
You are without pretension	Pasque Flower
You are young and beautiful	Red Rosebud
You make no pretension	Flora's Bell
You occupy my thoughts	Pansy; Purple Violet
You please all	Currants
You will be my death	Hemlock
Your image is engraved on my heart	Spindle Tree
Your presence revives me	Rosemary
Your wishes, success crown	Coronella

Youth	Early Primrose
Youthful gladness	Spring Crocus
Youthful love	Red Catchfly
Zealousness	Elder
Zest	Lemon

For a catalogue containing details of further books by Vernon Coleman please write to the publishers at Publishing House, Trinity Place, Barnstaple, Devon, EX32 9HJ, England.